The Amazing Incredible Shrinking Piano

Story by Thornton Cline
Illustrations by Susan Oliver

ISBN: 978-1-57424-318-5
SAN 683-8022

Cover by James Creative Group

All Illustrations by Susan Oliver

"Thornton Cline has given us another gem! With wit, humor, and a bit of fantasy, Cline weaves an important lesson into a delightful story that will entertain and motivate young musicians"

– Crystal Bowman, Best selling children's author of over 80 books

"A delightful story, The Amazing Incredible Shrinking Piano, teaches a valuable message on respect for musical instruments. Children will enjoy reading this story and singing the songs that are included again and again."

– Jennifer Foxx, Nationally recognized piano teacher/ clinician FPSResources.com

"An excellent book for aspiring musicians. Love your piano and it will love you back!"

– Daniel McFarlane, Australian composer of the Supersonics series for piano, in-demand teacher/clinician.

"Targeted at the most critical, formative period of a young musician's life, Thornton Cline's story is here to rescue a potentially disastrous musical moment and resonates truth with child-accessible simplicity. Yet, he doesn't stop there. Contained under the same cover, his original songs reinforce the moral lesson to children and adults alike, and provide additional motivation to rise to one's full potential."

– Michael Saltar, Epic composer, virtuoso pianist, orchestrator and scriptwriter

Lily was an adventurous girl.

She made her own kite and flew it in her backyard.

She built a castle out of tree limbs.

One day, Lily's grandmother visited her on her birthday. She said, "I have a surprise for you. I'm giving you my piano. I don't have room for it in my new apartment."

Lily shouted, "Thank you, Grandma!" She gave her a big hug.

"But, I don't know how to play."

"We will find you a piano teacher," her grandmother said.

After school that week, the piano movers
carried Lily's piano into her living room.

She tried her best to play but she sounded bad.

Lily slammed her hands against the keys making an awful sound.

She screamed, "I can't play this piano!"

Her mom wrapped her arms around her. She said, "Don't get upset Lily. How do you expect to play? You haven't taken any lessons. No matter how mad you get, you must never hit the piano. This piano was a gift from Grandma. I played it when I was your age."

Lily said, "I'm sorry, Mom."

The next week, Lily had her first piano lesson with Mr. Clark.

Mr. Clark taught her a new song. When Lily tried to play it she messed up.

She slammed her hands against the keys.

Mr. Clark stopped the lesson. There was silence. He said, "Lily you must never hit the piano, even if you get angry."

Lily said, "I'm sorry, Mr. Clark."

Weeks passed, Lily continued to show her anger when she made mistakes.

Her parents and Mr. Clark worried about her bad habit.

One night, when everyone was asleep, Lily had a dream. Her grandmother appeared in the dream and said, "Lily, I have given you my piano. It makes me sad to see you slam your hands against the keys. You're not listening to your parents or Mr. Clark. What you don't know is that this piano is no ordinary piano, it's magical. Every time you hit the piano it will shrink until you won't be able to play it."

The next day Lily told her friends at school her dream.

They said, "It's just a dream, don't worry."

Some of Lily's friends came over after school to hear Lily play piano.

Lily played her song perfectly until she messed up on the last few notes.

She slammed her hands against the keys and shouted, "I messed up!" Her friends stared at her. They were surprised she would hit her piano.

A few days later, when Lily tried to play her fingers couldn't fit on the keys because the keys were shrinking.

Each day she tried but the keys were getting smaller and smaller. They had become as small as tiny toy piano keys.

Lily was too embarrassed to tell her parents. She told Mr. Clark that she had too much homework to practice.

She told her friends.

They laughed and said, "No way, Lily, pianos don't shrink."

The next day at Lily's piano lesson she messed up. Mr. Clark stopped her and said, "Take a deep breath and count to ten. It will cool you down and you won't hit your piano again."

At home Lily thought about the dream and what her grandma had said.

Lily thought, *Maybe I should start treating my piano better.*

It was hard not to get mad when she played. Whenever she made a mistake she took a deep breath and counted to 10.

Weeks passed, Lily felt good. She was treating her piano better with kindness.

It was easier to play her songs than before. The keys had grown back to their original size.

On Mother's Day, Lily's grandmother came to visit. Lily played the piano.

"Lily, you sound great!" Grandma said.

Lily's mom said, "I'm proud of you."

Lily said, "I owe it all to a visitor in my dreams."

"Who?" Grandma asked.

"It's someone you know," Lily said.

Lily's grandma laughed and said, "Whatever you're doing, it's working."

Lily replied, "You know, Grandma, It doesn't pay to get mad at things—this piano is my best friend and I am going to be kind to it, even if I make a mistake."

THE END.

Song Titles

CD Track List

1. The Amazing Incredible Shrinking Piano (narration by Bryce Hitchcock)

2. The Amazing Incredible Shrinking Piano (narration by Bryce Hitchcock with page turn tones)

Children's Choir and Piano

3. I've Got A New Piano

4. My Piano Teacher

5. In My Dream

6. My Piano's Shrinking

7. Count to Ten

8. Piano and Friends

9. I Love To Play

10. My Mother and Granny

11. I Can Play My Piano Again

12. I Am Kind To My Piano

Piano Solos by Thornton Cline

13. I've Got A New Piano

14. My Piano Teacher

15. In My Dream

16. My Piano's Shrinking

17. Count to Ten

18. Piano and Friends

19. I Love to Play

20. My Mother and Granny

21. I Can Play My Piano Again

22. I Am Kind To My Piano

I've Got A New Piano

Thornton Cline

Cheerful ♩= 104

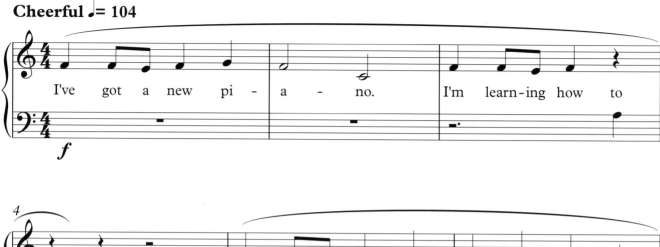

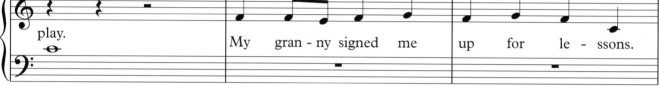

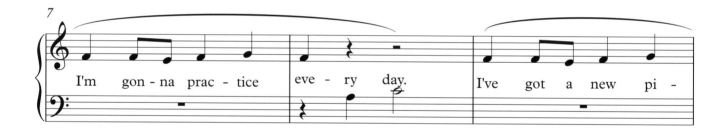

My Piano Teacher

Thornton Cline

Confidently ♩=92

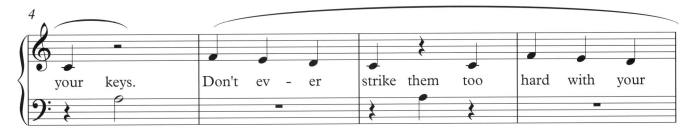

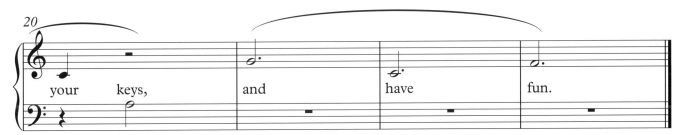

In My Dream

Thornton Cline

My Piano's Shrinking

Thornton Cline

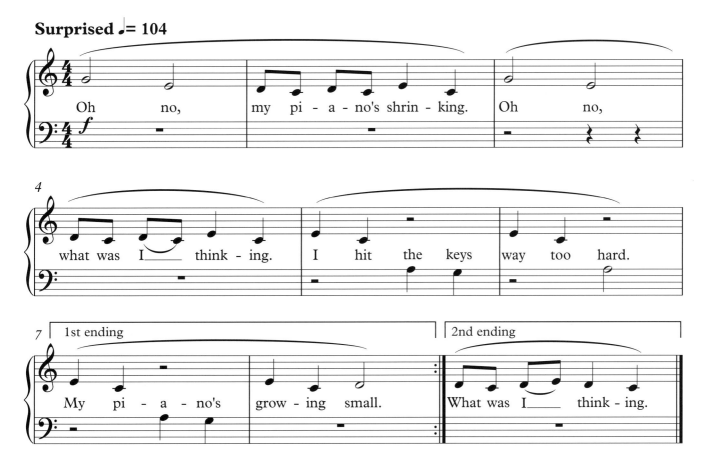

Count to Ten

Thornton Cline

Reflective ♩=96

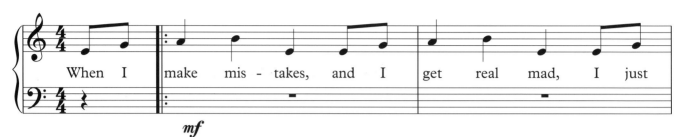

When I make mis - takes, and I get real mad, I just

mf

stop and hold my breath. And I count to ten, then I

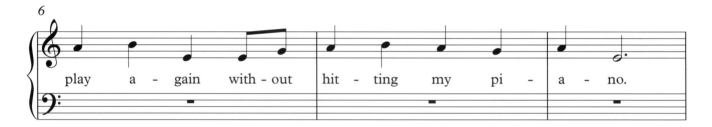

play a - gain with - out hit - ting my pi - a - no.

Fine

I don't want to hit my pi - a - no_. It is my best friend. When I

mp

D.C. al Fine

Piano and Friends

Thornton Cline

I Love to Play

Thornton Cline

Moderato ♩=92

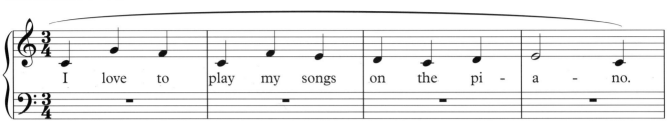

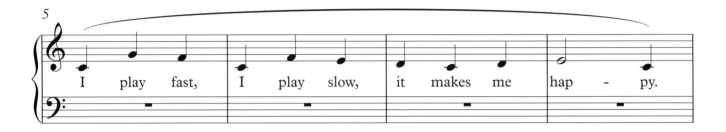

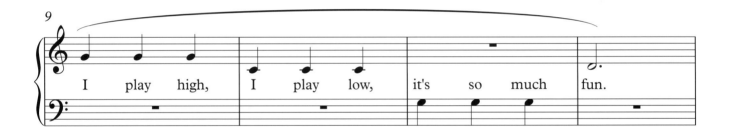

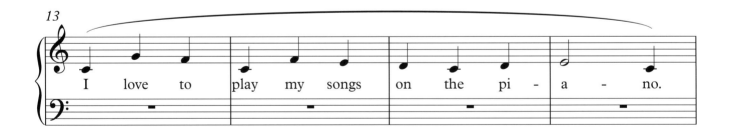

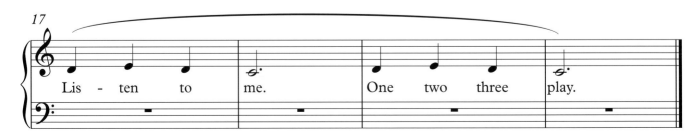

My Mother and Granny

I Can Play My Piano Again

Thornton Cline

I Am Kind to My Piano

Thornton Cline

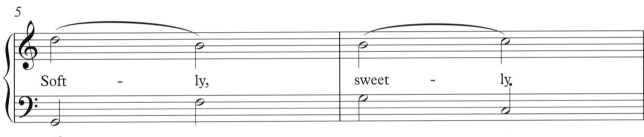

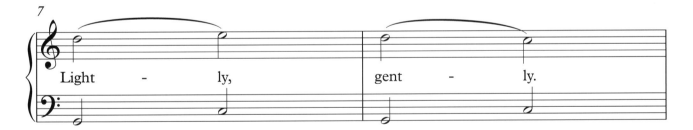

Biographies

Thornton Cline is author of five books: *Band of Angels, Practice Personalities: What's Your Type?, Practice Personalities for Adults, The Amazing Incredible Shrinking Violin* and Cline's second children's book, *The Amazing Incredible Shrinking Piano*. Thornton Cline has been honored with Songwriter of the Year twice in a row by the Tennessee Songwriters Association for his hit song "Love is the Reason" recorded by Engelbert Humperdinck and Gloria Gaynor. Cline has received Dove Award nominations and a Grammy nomination for music educator. Thornton Cline is an in-demand author, teacher, speaker, clinician, performer and songwriter. He is a registered Suzuki violin teacher with the Suzuki Association of Americas. Cline teachers piano, guitar, and violin at Cumberland University, Sumner Academy, Aaron Academy, Hendersonville Christian Academy, and at the Gallatin Creative Arts Center. He lives in Hendersonville, Tennessee with his wife Audrey and two children Mollie and Alex.

Susan Oliver is an award winning songwriter and visual artist as well as illustrator. She is originally from Orono, Maine and attended the University of Maine as well as Portland School of Art. Known for her wide variety of styles, Susan has exhibited her artwork and also worked as a graphic designer. Her painting, "Moonlight Seals" gained national attention in efforts to raise funds for Marine Animal Lifeline, an organization dedicated to seal rescue and rehabilitation. Susan now resides outside of Nashville, Tennessee where she continues to write music and design art work for album covers for various musical artists, as well as illustrates children's books. *The Amazing Incredible Shrinking Piano* is Oliver's second children's book published as an illustrator. She is illustrator of *The Amazing Incredible Shrinking Violin*.

Bryce Hitchcock is an actress/singer/songwriter from Nashville, Tennessee. She has voiced audiobooks, video games, film, TV and commercials. Most recently, she can be heard as the voice of "Deuce" in the new Final Fantasy Type-o HD video game just released in the US and Europe in March. She has done voice work for Disney, Sea World, Clear Channel and Tamagotchi commercials to name a few. Bryce has written many original songs including music for TV and film. Her sound is a blending of Folk, Blues, Jazz and Pop. You will find her performing a lot these days including venues like The House of Blues in San Diego and Los Angeles, Danny's in Venice, California, The Row and B. B. King's in Nashville, Tennessee. Bryce has returned from Ireland where she played a few of the local pubs and interviewed with radio stations.

Credits

Audrey Cline

Alex Cline

Mollie Cline

Roberta Cline

God

Ron Middlebrook

Clinetel Music

Centerstream Publishing

Hal Leonard

Susan Oliver, illustrator

Bryce Hitchcock, narrator

Lawrence Boothby, photographer

Crystal Bowman, editing

Marcelo Cataldo, musical transcriptions

Children's Choir:
  Libby P.
  Cohen T.
  Ethan K.
  Laura S.

Parents of children's choir

Sumner Academy

Cumberland Arts Academy

Cumberland University

Hendersonville Christian Academy

Gallatin Creative Arts Center

Aaron Academy

Another Great Shrinking Book!

THE AMAZING INCREDIBLE SHRINKING VIOLIN
Story by Thornton Cline, Illustrations by Susan Oliver
Young Austin begs his parents to play violin. But Austin doesn't make time to practice until one night he is visited by the violin fairy who warns him that if he doesn't practice his violin, it will shrink. Austin's classmates are amazed at what happens next! Austin discovers that if he wants to sound good, he must practice. This heartwarming story teaches the benefits of hard work and attaining one's goals. Austin's dream of becoming a big violin star is starting to come true. The book's whimsical illustrations by acclaimed illustrator Susan Oliver add to the charm and merriment of the story. The book includes a CD of 10 easy original songs for violin or voice (with lyrics sung by a children's choir) and narrations of the story. (Recommended for ages 4-8)
00142509 Book/CD Pack..$19.99

P.O. Box 17878 - Anaheim Hills, CA 92817
(714) 779-9390   www.centerstream-usa.com

More Great Books from Thornton Cline...

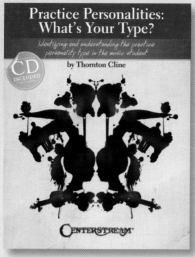

Did you like this book? If so, check out this great book!

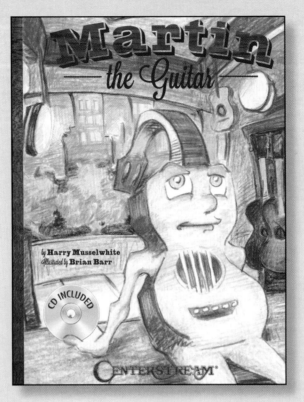

MARTIN THE GUITAR
by Harry Musselwhite

This charming children's story will delight music lovers of all ages. Little Martin the Guitar lives in Mr. Beninato's Music Store in New York City. He wants so much to be adopted and taken home by a fine musician, but the other larger instruments in the shop are always picked before him. Every night after Mr. Beninato goes home, all the instruments play for each other and compete for a place of honor in the shop. The large and loud guitar known as Big D always wins the contest. One night, Strada the Violin decides to step out of her special case and help Martin win the contest, and the two perform a duet that leaves the other instruments looking on with awe and admiration. Join Martin and all his friends for a CD of music from Mr. Beninato's Music Store! Performed on guitars, mandolins, banjos, and more, hear songs from the book entitled "Strada's Waltz," "Mr. Beninato's Music Shop," "Martin's Lullaby," and six more tunes made to bring a smile to your face and to set your toes tapping!

00001601 Book/CD Pack...$19.99

P.O. Box 17878 - Anaheim Hills, CA 92817
(714) 779-9390   www.centerstream-usa.com